ADAM ZAGAJEWSKI

UNSEEN HAND

TRANSLATED BY CLARE CAVANAGH

Adam Zagajewski was born in Lvov in 1945. His previous books include *Tremor, Canvas, Mysticism for Beginners, Without End, Two Cities, Another Beauty, A Defense of Ardor,* and *Eternal Enemies*—all published by FSG. He lives in Chicago and Krakow.

Clare Cavanagh is a professor of Slavic languages and literatures at Northwestern University. Her most recent book, *Lyric Poetry and Modern Politics*, received the National Book Critics Circle Award for criticism. She has also translated the poetry of Wislawa Szymborska.

UNSEEN HAND

ADAM ZAGAJEWSKI

TRANSLATED FROM

THE POLISH BY

CLARE CAVANAGH

FARRAR STRAUS GIROUX

NEW YORK

UNSEEN HAND

Farrar, Straus and Giroux

18 West 18th Street, New York 10011

Copyright © 2009 by Adam Zagajewski

Translation copyright © 2011 by Clare Cavanagh

Distributed in Canada by D&M Publishers, Inc.

Printed in the United States of America

Originally published in 2009 by Znak Publishers,

Poland, as *Niewidzialna ręka*

Published in the United States in 2011

by Farrar, Straus and Giroux

First American paperback edition, 2012

The Library of Congress has cataloged

the hardcover edition as follows:

Zagajewski, Adam, 1945–

    [Niewidzialna ręka. English.]

    Unseen hand / Adam Zagajewski ;

  translated by Clare Cavanagh. — 1st ed.

      p. cm.

    ISBN 978-0-374-28089-5 (alk. paper)

    I. Cavanagh, Clare. II. Title.

PG7185.A32 N5413 2011

891.8'5173—dc22

              2010046274

Paperback ISBN: 978-0-374-53336-6

Designed by Quemadura

www.fsgbooks.com

10 9 8 7 6 5 4 3 2 1

CONTENTS

III.

I.

NEW HOTEL

KRAKOW

In February the poplars are even slimmer
than in summer, frozen through. My family
spread across the earth, beneath the earth,
in different countries, poems, paintings.

Noon, I'm on Na Groblach Square.
I sometimes came to see my aunt
and uncle here (partly out of duty).
They'd stopped complaining about their fate,

the system, but their faces looked like
an empty secondhand bookshop.
Now someone else lives in that apartment,
strange people, the scent of a strange life.

A new hotel was built nearby,
bright rooms, breakfasts doubtless comme il faut,
juices, coffee, toast, glass, concrete,
amnesia—and suddenly, I don't know why,
a moment of penetrating joy.

CAFÉ

BERLIN

The café in a strange city bore a French writer's
name. I sat reading *Under the Volcano*,
with less enthusiasm now. Time to be healed,
I thought. I'd probably become a philistine.
Mexico was remote and its enormous stars
did not shine for me. The day of the dead dragged on.
Holiday of metaphors and light. Death played the lead.
A few people at neighboring tables, various fates.
Prudence, Sorrow, Common Sense. The Consul, Yvonne.
It was raining. I felt a little happiness. Someone entering,
someone leaving, someone had finally discovered the
    perpetuum mobile.
I was in a free country. A lonely country.
Nothing was happening, the cannons slept.
The music favored no one, pop seeped
from the speakers, lazily repeating: many events coming
    soon.
No one knew what to do, where to go, why.
I thought about you, our closeness, the scent
of your hair when autumn starts.

A plane rose from the airport
like a zealous pupil who believes
what the old masters told him.
The Soviet cosmonauts claimed they didn't find
God in outer space, but did they look?

VITA CONTEMPLATIVA

It may already be September. I drank tasteless coffee
in a café garden on Museumsinsel
and thought about Berlin, its dark waters.
These black buildings have seen much.
But peace reigns in Europe, diplomats doze,
the sun is pale, summer dies serenely,
spiders weave its shining shroud, the dry leaves
of plane trees write memoirs of their youth.

So this is the *vita contemplativa*.
The Pergamon's dark walls, white sculptures inside.
A bust of Greek loveliness. So this is it.
An altar before which no one prays.
So this is the *vita contemplativa*.
Happiness. A moment without an hour, in the words
of the poet killed in Lublin by a bomb. So this is it.
And what if, in this or another city, the *vita activa*
burst forth once more, what would Artemis,
fourth century B.C.E., do? Narcissus? Hermes?

Pergamon faces watch me with envy
—I still make mistakes, they can't.

Comparing day and night; so this is it.

Dream with waking, world and mind. Joy.

Composure, focus, the heart's levitation.

Bright thoughts smolder in dark walls.

So this is it. What we do not know.

We live in the abyss. In dark waters. In brightness.

FIRST COMMUNION

Dark gray houses and triangular bay windows,
near a little park with German statues
(pseudo-baroque from the thirties).
Mrs. Kolmer took my picture there
right after my First Communion
against the backdrop of a freshly laundered sheet:
I'm that chubby child. Earnest,
upright, candle in hand.
I'm a beginning Catholic,
who struggles to tell good from evil,
but doesn't know what divides them,
especially at dawn and dusk, when
for a long moment the light wavers.
The poplar leaves in the garden are black,
the light is black, the homes are black,
the air's transparent, only the sheet is white.
Color photos will come later
to mute the contrasts and perhaps permit
an ordinary life, splendid holidays,
even a second communion.

LUXEMBOURG GARDENS

Parisian apartment houses fear neither wind nor
    imagination—
they're solid paperweights,
the antithesis of dreaming.

White boats race the river, packed with crowds
demanding greetings from the shore-bound;
their champagne mood liquidates the past.

A pair of wealthy tourists emerges from a cab
in gleaming outfits; waiters serve them
wearing frock coats whose cut is untouched by fashion.

But the Luxembourg Gardens grow empty now,
and become a vast, quiet herbarium;

they don't recall all those who once
strolled their avenues, who haven't noticed that they're dead.

Mickiewicz lived here, and over there August Strindberg
sought the philosopher's stone
he never found.

Dusk falls. Sober night approaches from the east,
taciturn and troubled.
Night comes from Asia, and asks no questions.

Foreignness is splendid, a cold pleasure.
Yellow lights illuminate the windows on the Seine
(there's the real mystery: the life of others).

I know—the city no longer holds secrets.
But there are plane trees, squares, cafés, friendly streets,
and the bright gaze of clouds that slowly dies.

OUT WALKING WITH MY FATHER

GRUNWALD SQUARE, GLIWICE

My father remembers next to nothing. With slight exceptions.

Do you remember fixing transmitters for the Home Army?

Of course I remember. Were you afraid?

I don't remember. Was mother afraid? I don't know.

The garden on Piaskowa Street? Sure.

The scent of linden blossoms? No.

Do you remember Mr. Romer? Sometimes.

Skiing on Czantoria Mountain? I guess not.

Do you remember infinity? No, I don't.

But I'll see it soon. (He *could* say that.)

JOSEPH STREET IN WINTER

FOR JOACHIM RUSSEK

In winter Joseph Street is dark,
a few pilgrims flounder through wet snow
and don't know where they're going, to which star,
and maybe they stop short
like the gardener, who leans
against his shovel handle, dreaming,
and doesn't see that war
has unexpectedly erupted
or that the hydrangea has bloomed.

THE LOVELY GARONNE

FOR AGNÈS AND PATRICE MOYON

Because you didn't flow through my childhood.
Because I didn't swim in your currents.
Because even now, beneath the archaeologist's hand
the same helmet grows, and the ancient swastika
of a worse Rome. Because you might have been
my sister, my prison, my
salvation, the happiness of a summer day.
Because you are memory, and your
vowels sing a song
that we don't want to understand.

I DREAMED OF MY CITY

WRITTEN WHILE ATTENDING
A HERBERT CONFERENCE IN SIENA

I dreamed of my distant city—
it spoke the language of children and the injured,
it spoke in many voices, rushing
to shout one another down, like simple people suddenly
    admitted
to the presence of a great official:
"There is no justice," it cried; "All
has been taken from us," it wailed loudly;
"No one remembers us, not a soul";
I saw feminists with dark eyes,
petty nobles with forgotten family trees,
judges wearing togas sewn of nettles
and devout, exhausted Jews—

                              but slowly, relentlessly
the gray dawn drew near and the speakers faded,
dimmed, submissively went back to their barracks
like legions of toy soldiers,
and then I heard completely different words:

"Still there are miracles, not everyone believes,
but miracles do happen . . ." And waking, slowly,
reluctantly departing the dream's bunker,
I realized that the arguments continue,
that nothing has been settled yet . . .

PIANO LESSON

Piano lesson at the neighbors', Mr. and Mrs. J.
I'm in their apartment for the first time,
which smells different from ours (ours has no smell,
or so I think). Everywhere carpets,
thick Persian carpets. I know that they're Armenians,
but don't know what that means. Armenians have carpets,

dust wanders through the air, imported
from Lvov, medieval dust.
We don't have carpets or Middle Ages.
We don't know who we are—maybe wanderers.
Sometimes I think we don't exist. Only others are.
The acoustics are great in our neighbors' apartment.

It's quiet in this apartment. A piano stands in the room
like a lazy, tamed predator—and in it,
at its very heart, dwells music's black ball.
Mrs. J told me right after the first
or second lesson that I should take up languages
since I showed no talent for music.

I show no talent for music.
I should take up languages instead.
Music will always be elsewhere,
inaccessible, in someone else's apartment.
The black ball will be hidden elsewhere,
but there may be other meetings, revelations.

I went home, hanging my head,
a little saddened, a little glad—home,
where there was no smell of Persia, only amateur paintings,
watercolors, and I thought with bitterness and pleasure
that I had only language, only words, images,
only the world.

DEFENSELESS

IN MEMORIAM PAOLA MALAVASI

September 2005, we came back from vacation,
sat down at the kitchen table
covered in green oilcloth.
Suddenly Nicola calls, asking, do you know
that Paola Malavasi died
suddenly, in the morning,
on Sunday, at a hotel in Venice.
No, I hadn't heard—those two words,
died and *Paola*, met then
for the first time.
                    Paola had
just turned forty,
a pretty, smiling woman.
She taught Greek and Latin at the high school,
she wrote and translated poems.
The word *died* is much older
and never smiles.
Some months have passed,
and I still don't believe in her death.
Paola studied life and poetry,

antiquity and today.

Nothing speaks to her death.

She seems serene in the photographs,

her face is defenseless and open.

Her face still summons the future,

but the future, distracted,

now looks the other way.

FAMILY HOME

You come here like a stranger,
but this is your family home.
The currants, the apple and cherry trees don't know you.
One noble tree readies
a new brood of walnuts in peace,
while the sun, like a worried first-grader,
diligently colors in the shadows.
The dining room pretends it is a crypt,
and doesn't give out one familiar echo—
the old conversations haven't lingered.
There, where your life doubtless
began, someone else's television stutters.
But the cellar's been collecting darknesses—
all the nights since you left
are snarled like the yarn of an old sweater
in which wild cats have nested.
You come here like a stranger,
but this is your family home.

MUTE CITY

Imagine a dark city.
It understands nothing. Silence reigns.
And in the quiet bats like Ionian philosophers
make sudden, radical decisions in mid-flight,
filling us with admiration.
Mute city. Blanketed in clouds.
Nothing is known yet. Nothing.
Sharp lightning cleaves the night.
Priests, Catholic and Orthodox alike, rush to shroud
their windows in deep blue velvet,
but we go out
to hear the rain's rustle
and the dawn. Dawn always tells us something,
always.

SELF-PORTRAIT IN AN AIRPLANE

IN ECONOMY CLASS

Crouched like an embryo,
crushed into the narrow seat,
I try to remember
the scent of fresh-cut hay
when wooden carts descend
in August from the mountain meadows,
lurching down dirt roads
and the driver cries out
as men always do when they panic
—they screamed that way in the *Iliad*
and have never fallen silent since,
not during the Crusades,
or later, much later, near us,
when no one listens.

I'm tired, I think about what
can't be thought—about the silence that reigns
in forests when the birds sleep,
about the coming end of summer.
I hold my head in my hands

as if shielding it from annihilation.
Seen from outside I doubtless
seem immobile, almost dead,
resigned, deserving sympathy.
But it's not so—I'm free,
maybe even happy.
Yes, I hold my heavy head
in my hands,
but inside it a poem is being born.

LEONARDO

He lives in France now,
calmer and much weaker.
He is the jewel in the crown. Favored
with the monarch's friendship.
The Loire rolls its waters slowly.
He considers the projects
he left unfinished.
His right hand, half-paralyzed,
has already departed.
His left would also like to take its leave.
And his heart, and his whole body.
Islands of light still
stand sentry.

ON A BENCH

You sit on a bench, leafing through Benn's poems
—noisy streets around you, an airplane overhead,
the president-elect smiles uncertainly (it's just a poster).

Children play in the sandbox,
someone draws water from a rusty well
(a rowan tree on the lawn—farther off the Art Exhibit Bureau).

You turn pages scored with black lava
and await the signal—who's won, the living city
or the shadow of the poet long since gone,

but at last silence comes, calmness—
unexpectedly, from unknown quarters, there appears
that je ne sais quoi you know so well.

JUNE IN SIENA

—we shall never be in touch with something
greater than ourselves **— RICHARD RORTY**

Flat days came to pass, when doubt governed,
days of obvious accord.

Summer cried loudly like vegetable sellers
in Parisian markets.

Lovers, spliced together on benches, began to tally
future gains and losses,

months of happiness and contention.

June in Siena: on every small square the boys
practiced their kettledrums before the Palio—

the brown city quivered like troops before a battle.
Dry lips waited for rain.

WHEN FATHER HIKED

When father hiked through the mountains, tireless,
patient, sometimes for hours in the rain,
under his cape, like bygone pilgrims
trudging toward Spain, I thought
that yes, of course, he'd cross the mild slopes
and come one day to the other side,
but I failed to account for sudden
shifts in the terrain, the treacherous drops
that always accompany
the trails dotted with signposts for tourists,
white, sky-blue, or red;
the chasms have no color,
shadows dwell there, and blackberries grow,
sweet only in autumn.

IMPOSSIBLE

5414 S. BLACKSTONE, CHICAGO

It's so hard, trying to write, be it
at home, on a plane above the ocean,
over a black forest, in the evening stillness.
Always starting fresh, reaching
full speed and fifteen minutes later
giving up, in reluctant surrender.
I hope that you at least can hear me,
—since, as you know, the theoreticians remind us
insistently, almost daily, that we've missed
the point, as usual we've skipped
the deeper meaning, we've been reading
the wrong books, alas,
we've drawn the wrong conclusions.
They claim: poetry is fundamentally impossible,
a poem is a hall where faces dissolve
in a golden haze of spotlights, where the fierce
rumblings of an angry mob drown out
defenseless single voices.
So what then? Fine words perish quickly,
ordinary words rarely persuade.

All the evidence suggests *silentium*
claims only a handful of adherents.
Sometimes I envy the dead poets,
they no longer have "bad days," they don't know
"ennui," they've parted ways with "vacancy,"
"rhetoric," rain, low-pressure zones,
they've stopped following the "shrewd reviews,"
but they keep speaking to us.
Their doubts vanished with them,
their rapture lives.

JANUARY 27

Frosty day. A winter sun. White breath.
But on this Friday we didn't know
what to celebrate and what to mourn—
it was Holocaust Memorial Day
and Mozart's birthday.
Our memory was perplexed.
Our imagination lost its way.
The candle on the windowsill wept
(we'd been asked to light candles),
but the gentle music of young Mozart
reached us from the speakers, rococo,
the age of silver wigs and not the gray hair
we knew from Auschwitz,
the age of costumes, not of nakedness,
hope and not despair.
Our memory was perplexed,
our imagination grew lost in thought.

3 ARKONSKA STREET

IN GLIWICE

Mrs. Mazonska was our neighbor from the first floor
at 3 Arkonska Street (Pszoniak lived next door,
Różewicz on the corner of Zygmunt and Słowacki).
She had dyed red hair and gold on her fingers.
Her husband, a tall, thin professor at the Polytechnic,
gave me albums full of stamps,
with a green Congo, a sky-blue France,
and a few pinkish brown Second Republics.
Mrs. Mazonska invited me sometimes
for tea and treated me like a grown-up,
with serious, straightforward conversation.
But I wasn't really grown-up.
I didn't know who I was—
in the mirror I saw only eyes
that didn't look at me.
Chestnuts fell from the trees, shining and pure.
Beyond the window, in the grass, in the microscopic garden,
quizzical starlings hopped.
In the church tower, and the town hall tower, on the walls

of our apartments, in flat wristwatches,
time worked relentlessly;
it was ubiquitous—the secret police
were no match for it,
even thought couldn't keep up.

THE REVOLUTION HAS ENDED

REMEMBERING JULIAN KORNHAUSER'S
MOURNFUL REVOLUTIONARIES

The revolution has ended. In the parks pedestrians
marched slowly, dogs traced perfect circles,
as if guided by an unseen hand.
The weather was lovely, rain like diamonds,
women in summer dresses, children as always
slightly peeved, peaches on tabletops.
An old man sat in a café and cried.
Sports car motors roared,
newspapers shrieked, and essentially, it should be said,
life revealed ascendant tendencies
—to employ a neutral definition,
thus wounding neither victors nor the vanquished,
or those who still didn't know
which side they were on,
that is, in effect, all of us
who write or read these words.

II.

THE BOTANIC GARDEN

In the Krakow Botanic Garden
I came upon an Asiatic tree
bearing the name *Chinese Metasequoia*—a lovely tree
with ragged, palmate needle-leaves.
But why metasequoia—not just a regular sequoia?

Does the metasequoia grow beyond itself?
Does it tower above the other trees?
Have even plants begun to draw upon
the arcane jargon
of certain academic sages?

LOST

Lost, lost in gray hallways.
At night the lightbulbs hiss like signals of sinking ships.
We read books forgotten by their authors.
There is no truth, wise men repeat.
Summer evenings: festivals of swifts,
peonies erupting in the suburbs.
Streets seem abbreviated
by the heat, the ease of seeing.
Autumn creeps up surreptitiously.
Still sometimes we surface for a moment,
and the setting sun sometimes gleams
and a short-lived certainty appears,
nearly faith.

JOSEPH STREET

I often walk down Joseph Street, I enter Joseph's dreams,
always seeking to detect where that peculiar
street leads; it turns where
there is nothing, and I wonder what I am,
a passerby who won't last long.
The happiness and sorrow gathered here will save
no one, although the harvest may be abundant.
Years pass, I remain, memory is uncertain,
unheard prayers lie underfoot,
sparrows are eternity's frail emblem,
the rain is only recollection, the silhouettes
of unknown persons walk without casting shadows.
Toward evening the light grows feebler and death
rides swiftly on its high cart, laughing.

CORRIDOR

FOR RUTH AND MARIA BUCZYŃSKI

I liked the comic rituals of young poets,
the panicked moments, the anxieties
before the reading, the slow passage
through a dark corridor toward the lighted stage,
performing poems to a drowsy
public that woke up now and then,
the great and lesser envies and the moment when
the inarguable charm of one good line,
an unexpected metaphor or image meant
that all was—temporarily—forgiven.
Sometimes someone would ask uncertainly—
but won't you tell us how to live?
—I thought it was funny then, but not now.
I liked the silence not without
its deeper meanings, the jokes, the chats
with timid readers and finally
the signing of the books with the names
that we knew, without question,
truly belonged to us.

AND THE LOVELY GARONNE

Geh aber nun und grüsse
Die schöne Garonne

—FRIEDRICH HÖLDERLIN

And the lovely Garonne. Among castles and when it vanishes
in caves without echoes or mirrors.
And still it returns to light, to air.
At dusk its waters work attentively
—great factories of invisibility.
The streams tell it about storms
and about completely quiet, peaceful days,
when time sways on the meadows
like happy schoolboys playing hooky.
And the lovely Garonne. And our life, which weaves
between hills dotted with olive trees,
unprepossessing willows, still their fruit sustains us.
Above it a rosy city rises—at night
it turns gray like the eyes of vagrants.

Finally ships reach the harbor,
trains attain the station terminus
(with its buffet and its stout, good-natured waitress);

life dwindles, and we still don't know,
we still understand nothing.
And the lovely Garonne parts with the vineyards
and goshawks, who are not entirely bad,
but it doesn't cry, although the ocean's
white-green expanse gleams ahead
and even its name will be erased
and the waves will hold only little clumps,
the whispers of a river that is no more.
And it will be said: the lovely Garonne has gone.
But it flows on and on and on.

THE LAST STOP

The tram rumbled past red houses.
The wheels in mining towers whirled
like carousels in fairgrounds.
Roses dimmed by soot grew in the gardens,
wasps raged in pastry shops
above cakes strewn with crumbs.
I was fifteen, the tram moved
quicker between the housing projects,
in the meadows I spotted marsh marigolds.
I thought that at the last stop
the meaning of it all would stand revealed,
but nothing happened, nothing,
the driver ate a roll with cheese,
two old women talked quietly
about prices and diseases.

NOW THAT YOU'VE
LOST YOUR MEMORY

TO MY FATHER

Now that you've lost your memory
and can only smile, defenseless,
I want to help—it was you,
after all, who opened my imagination like a demiurge.
I remember our excursions, woolly clouds
swimming low over a damp mountain forest
(you knew every path in those woods), and
the summer day when we scaled the heights
of a lighthouse above the Baltic
and we watched the endless rippling of the sea,
its white stitches frayed like basted seams.
I won't forget that moment, I think you were
moved too—we seemed to see the whole world,
boundless, calmly breathing, blue and perfect,
at once distinct and hazy, near and distant;
we felt the planet's roundness, we heard the gulls,
who played at aimless gliding
through warm and chilly currents of the air.
I can't help you, I have only one memory.

SELF-PORTRAIT IN

A LITTLE MUSEUM

A swarthy Christ watched me
from small trecento paintings;
I didn't understand his gaze,
but I wanted to open up before it.
A rapt, darked-haired Christ,
unswervingly attentive,
bounded by Byzantium's gold frame,
watched me while my thoughts
were elsewhere—
I followed, with growing vexation,
an elderly couple, French:
in the quiet museum, nearly empty,
he read out loud, too loud,
from the appropriate page in the guidebook.

MUSIC OF THE LOWER SPHERES

I'M WALKING DOWN KARMELICKA STREET

Sparrows on the windowsill; rain is coming.

In the demolished church nettles proclaimed a plebeian gospel.

Only you, light.

"Lili Marlene": the melody caught me from a passing car.

You sought and didn't find: you found and didn't seek.

October: mild evenings, early dusk—

efforts continue before the arrival of winter.

The black-and-white cat was called M.

Spain's stars spoke feverishly, but no one listened.

You're in an airplane, trapped in your seat, but with eyes open.

The continent shifts slowly, like a fan.

Perhaps Plotinus is among the passengers, a timid clerk.

I'll never see you again.

On the beach: a lazy ocean greets the earth and leaves at once.

You're no longer young, he said with a certain satisfaction.

The December night gulps shadows.

A stationer's—the scent of childhood.

Snow circled above the houses, the pigeons watched with envy.

After so many catastrophes—but they eat breakfast, take a rest.

"Plotinus was ashamed to have a body."

At dusk soldiers in unbuttoned uniforms drank beer.

She loved Mallarmé with blind devotion.

They don't like you, R says.

Look, the train from Vienna seeks a path between brown hills.

The girl handing out flyers instantly pinpointed the age of passersby.

Poster: *Course in last things. Foreign instructors. Discount for students.*

I know only this: it exists, even if it disappears.

I'm in a room, trapped in an armchair, but my mind is free.

Free, but not lonely.

Strawberry ice cream melts on the asphalt.

If I could only open my heart.

THE GREAT POET HAS GONE

THINKING OF C.M.

Of course nothing changes
in the ordinary light of day,
when the great poet has gone.
Gray sparrows and dapper starlings
still squabble heatedly
in the tops of ancient elms.

When the great poet has gone,
the city doesn't miss a beat, the metro
and the trams still seek a modern Grail.
In the library a lovely girl
looks in vain for a poem that could explain it all.

At noon the same noise surges,
while quiet concentration reigns at night,
among the stars—eternal agitation.
Soon the discotheques will open,
indifference will open—
although the great poet has died.

When we part for a long while
or forever from someone we love,
we suddenly sense there are no words,
we must speak for ourselves now,
there's no one to do it for us
—since the great poet is gone.

LIKE THE KING OF ASINI

Like the King of Asini in Seferis—I thought,
remembering the great poem:
the heat, the quiet sea, oblivion beneath a golden mask,
two people in a kayak, mute cliffs,
a massive world, and on the other side only
"Asini" and its master—a single word in the *Iliad*,
the shortest entry in the catalogue of ships . . .

I too have sought the absent—
in so many cities, on an airplane, in the ruins
of failed uprisings, confederations,
during the failed trip to Syracuse,
on long walks through Paris,
on the coast of an ocean where
a continent would drown.

Like the King of Asini in Seferis, I thought—
nothing beneath the gold mask, a living absence—
but that void may be filled
at any moment, it may happen

that the king will suddenly return and gold will shine
   triumphant.
Damp gooseberry bushes rustle in the garden,
the wind stirs. Know that we're waiting.
We're still waiting.

SEPTEMBER EVENING

YES, IN LVOV

The white church of the Carmelites on a low hill
and right beside it Franciscan Street, where my
grandfather was once the stern director of a school
(he grew kinder only with age).
Heaps of stones, the pockmarked pavement,
as if someone had been hunting treasure.
Yellow leaves cling to the gaunt trees,
cautiously, without conviction.
This is the building they entered,
and the gate that likes only shadows.
But now there's nothing anyway, just me,
shivering from the cold, and the empty September evening.
I must jot down a few words so that winter
may chew its black bread of forgetting.

RAVENNA

MAY 2006

This sleepy little town was once an empire's capital.
This baker was an imperial baker.
This fire flamed high.
This tailor hunched over cloth of gold.
This oriole sang in the language of the gods.

Ravenna is quiet, botanical.
Thrushes stroll across the flat earth.
Bicycles chat familiarly, like deaf-mutes.
A lazy train from Ferrara draws into the station,
two German ladies argue: How is *solitude* pronounced?

These bricks touched fingers.
These fingers touched trees and metal.
These acacias reached to Roman arches.
A Ravenna bookmark lies, a little bored,
in a herbarium of guidebooks.

A golden flame still smolders in mosaics;
it will doubtless flicker out one day.

But one match will do
to revive it.
One moment of attention.
Or will it?

ABOUT MY MOTHER

I could never say anything about my mother:
how she repeated, you'll regret it one day,
when I'm not around anymore, and how I didn't believe
in either "I'm not" or "anymore,"
how I liked watching as she read bestsellers,
always turning to the last chapter first,
how in the kitchen, convinced it wasn't
her proper place, she made Sunday coffee,
or, even worse, filet of cod,
how she studied the mirror while expecting guests,
making the face that best kept her
from seeing herself as she was (I take
after her in this and other failings),
how she went on at length about things
that weren't her strong suit and how I stupidly
teased her, for example, when she
compared herself to Beethoven going deaf,
and I said, cruelly, but you know he
had talent, and how she forgave it all
and how I remember that, and how I flew from Houston
to her funeral and couldn't say anything
and still can't.

SMALL SELF-PORTRAIT (JUNE)

KRAKOW, WASHINGTON AVENUE

Just as in dreams, in dreams—I told myself.
It was early June, all the birds were singing,
the world overflowed with scents and voices;
the lilacs were over now, but the acacias
proudly took their place, and the jasmine
was next in line;
the ash leaves (ash trees—my first love!)
immaculately frail and green.
I walked along the avenue down to the town,
familiar and friendly,
and I felt the great happiness of the living,
the happiness lent us
at ruinous rates by the Gypsies
(hidden Gypsies, proud and unforgiving).

NEXT SPRING

The nations were exhausted after many wars
and lay serenely in their marriage beds
vast as the Danube river basin.
Spring had begun, the first ecstasies.
In the boughs of trees, still naked,
Turkish turtle doves were cooing.
No one knew what to do, what to think.
We were orphans, since winter
had left us no testament;
a young butterfly studied flying
haphazardly, from scratch.
Butterflies lack tradition.
But we must die.
This is an inelegant
way to end a poem,
R protests. And adds:
A poem should end
better than a life. That's the point.

PIANO TUNER

AT THE CHICAGO PHILHARMONIC

At intermission a man in a corduroy jacket
emerges from backstage, lays his hands on the piano like
an experienced obstetrician, and vanishes, while the heedless
audience breathes deeply. We're alive, the musicians say.
    We're listening,
say the elegant ladies. And the performance continues,
    although the night
has long since seized the city's strategic points and
    Venus shines
with its cold beam.

METAPHOR

Every metaphor is a failure, said
the very old poet in the hotel bar,
turning to his rapt pupils.
The very old poet was in fine form
and said, with a wineglass in his hand:
It's the fundamental problem of incarnation,
the things we love, the unseen things,
take flesh, of course, in what can
be seen and said, though never
absolutely, one to one,
so it follows that there's always a little too much
or a little too little, the seams remain on the surface,
fingers jut, buttons, umbrellas, fingernails,
uncollected letters in azure airmail envelopes,
the sense of shortfall or excess remains,
someone is ominously silent, someone else
summons help, the ice cracks, the ambulance
arrives, too late, alas, but just wait,
thanks to this, thanks to this incongruity,
thanks to this inexplicable rupture,
we may keep chasing the chimera of metaphor,
all our lives we walk in darkness,

in a dim forest, we track the trail of simile,
imperfect, just like my
speech, just now reaching
its conclusion, although there is
no doubt much more to add,
but I fear that I'm already
growing weary and seem
to hear sleep calling.

WALL

IN MEMORIAM HENRYK BERESKA

He always seemed young,
caught up in new projects and proposals;
he worked nonstop.
He liked to talk about the window
in his last apartment,
the East Berlin window that looked out
all those years on the wall and the West,
that enigmatic land, forbidden.
The wall covered in snow, in frost,
slick and damp with rain in May,
darkening in autumn;
the wall—a thing unto itself,
the jewel of German idealist philosophy.
When *die Wende* arrived, the turning point,
Henryk got even younger—
and decided to start a new life,
the life of a free man,
citizen of a free country.
He couldn't understand those
who mourned the end of the dictatorship.

He was full of tempered ardor,
though his neighbor in the village
where he kept his summer house,
an ex–Stasi officer, failed to stir
his sympathies. Of course.
He traveled through Europe, in Poland
honors and awards awaited him.
It seemed he would live on,
that he'd be given extra years
to reward him for that East Berlin window.
But a different decision was made. A different verdict.
Neither reward nor punishment,
just frost, snow, and mist.

NOT THINKING ABOUT AESTHETICS

When, in the eighties, my father copied out
my poem "To Go to Lvov" for friends
(he told me about it much later,
with some embarrassment), I doubt he was thinking about
    aesthetics,
metaphors, stresses, deeper meanings,
only about the city he'd loved and lost, the city
where his early years, his epiphanies, his meetings with
    the world
had been detained like hostages,
and he must have struck the keyboard of his faithful old
typewriter with such force that if we
better understood the conservation of energy,
we might perhaps regenerate
on this basis at least one street
of his first rapture.

FALLING ASLEEP OVER

A VOLUME OF CAVAFY

Late evening, after a hard day,
falling asleep over a volume of Cavafy
in an armchair well acquainted with my frailties
(and occasional inspired moments),
I saw those men, old and young,
who endured failure superbly, with grace,
and accepted the catastrophe of their nations, their cities
(systematically subdued by Rome),
not easily, but with unequaled
brilliance—their consolation came in speech,
the peerless, plastic speech of the *Iliad* or Sophocles,
along with something no conquest could take from them
(or so they thought):
their place in the Hellenic world.
Thus Myris, Aimilianos, the poet Phernazis,
also a certain prince from western Libya,
not to mention the famous Antony,
who bade a brave farewell to Alexandria,
or the comic, clumsy Julian
(who could have been a Communist agitator).

All of them—except improper Julian—
were taken up with preparations
for eternal rest, a beautified defeat;
and almost all stir our sympathy,
though few of them are heroes
(cunning, not honor, drives them).
While our drowsiness is, after all, just
a trifling sketch, a foretaste of a greater whole
(as editors of literary supplements say).
Our defeats still doze
(or so at least it seems),
while the last passersby return
to their narrow apartments,
at night, when the heart beats slower
and the thick, gray smoke of the quotidian
flees the chimney like a ghost
(our life burns).

POETS PHOTOGRAPHED

Poets photographed,
but never when
they truly see,
poets photographed
against a backdrop of books,
but never in darkness,
never in silence,
at night, in uncertainty,
when they hesitate,
when joy, like phosphorus,
clings to matches.
Poets smiling,
well-informed, serene.
Poets photographed
when they're not poets.
If only we knew
what music is.
If only we understood.

IMPASSIVE

And the impassive Garonne flowed in silence
like an Indian brave in plumes of sun.
No one saw, no cameras,
only an azure eye; absolute ignorance,
serenity, glory, bliss.
A letter opener
lay on the wooden table,
a handful of nuts, a purple plum
that shone violet
as in a Spanish canvas,
a worn-out plastic ballpoint
with dark streaks of poetry.
Is it a memory
or the promise of new life?

SWIFTS STORMING

ST. CATHERINE'S CHURCH

Watching the swifts storm St. Catherine's Church,
its lofty walls raised of brick and white stone
—an unfinished basilica, earthquakes
and fires beset it, the transept
and tower were never built—I thought:
the swifts in their mad, haphazard, grand
attack on the Gothic structure and in their whistles,
shrill and coarse, utterly un-human,
competing with cell ringtones
and singing blackbirds, giving their final concert,
are the image of ecstasy, but not ecstasy itself,
they can't be, they don't want to be—
they aren't John of the Cross or Catherine of Alexandria
or Catherine of Siena, they know neither fullness nor void,
doubt and pursuit, despair and rapture.
These swifts are of the species *Apus apus*,
they resemble swallows but share
no kinship, they're unable
to navigate on land, they know only one thing—flight,
only the endless soaring overhead

that demands a spectator both slightly sober
and a little touched, they need an eye and a heart;
the eye must trace the trajectories of dark missiles,
the trail of a spaceship smashed
into tiny shards of dark nervous matter,
and the heart must sustain them with what it cannot
lack, enthusiasm, and thus fortified,
the swifts and the observer's heart join for a brief moment
in an unlikely contract, in admiration
for a world that has decided on a late June evening,
so it seems, to reveal before us, nonchalantly,
one of its zealously kept secrets
before night returns, mosquitoes and ignorance,
and my life, unfinished, uncertain,
made of joy and fear, of ceaseless,
unsated curiosity, what's coming next;
but now the day's shutters bang closed
(and I've already said too much).

FACES

Evening on the market square I saw shining faces
of people I didn't know. I looked greedily
at people's faces: each was different,
each said something, persuaded,
laughed, endured.

I thought that the city is built not of houses,
squares, boulevards, parks, wide streets,
but of faces gleaming like lamps,
like the torches of welders, who mend
steel in clouds of sparks at night.

III.

UNWRITTEN ELEGY

FOR KRAKOW'S JEWS

My family lived here for five hundred years —DR. M.S.

But Joseph Street is the saddest, spare as a new moon,
not a single tree though not without charm,
the dark charm of a province, of parting, a quiet burial;
in the evening shadows gather here from every neighborhood,
and even some brought by trains from nearby towns.
Joseph was the Lord's favorite, but his street knew no
    happiness,
no pharaoh distinguished it, its dreams were sorrowful,
    its years were lean.

In the Church of Corpus Christi I lit candles for my dead,
who live far off—I don't know where
—and I sense they warm themselves in the red flame too,
like the homeless by a fire when the first snow falls.
I walk the paths of Kazimierz and think of those who are
    missing.
I know that the eyes of the missing are like water and can't
be seen—you can only drown in them.

To hear footsteps in the evening—and see no one.

They walk on, although there's no one here, the tread of
women in boots

shod with iron, beside the hangman's quiet, almost tender
steps.

What is it? As if black memory moves

above the city, like a comet withdrawing from the
stratosphere.

IMPROVISATION

First you take the world's whole weight on yourself
and make it light, bearable.
Toss it on your shoulders
like a backpack and take to the road.
Best at evening, in the spring, when
trees breathe peacefully and the night promises
to be fine, in the garden elm branches crackle.
The whole weight? Blood and ugliness? Can't be done.
A taste of bitterness always stays in the mouth
and the contagious despair of the old woman
you saw yesterday in the tram.
Why lie? Rapture, after all,
lives only in imagination and quickly vanishes.
Improvisation—always just improvisation,
we know nothing else, small or large—
in music, when the jazz trumpet weeps gaily,
or when you look at a white sheet of paper
or also when you flee
from sorrow and open a favorite book of poems,
the telephone usually rings right then
and someone asks, would you consider, sir or ma'am,
our latest models? No, thank you.

Grayness and monotony remain; mourning
that the finest elegy can't heal.
Perhaps, though, there are hidden things before us
and in them sorrow blends with enthusiasm,
always, daily, like the birth of dawn
on the seashore, or no, hold on,
like the happy laughter of the two little altar boys
in white surplices, on the corner of Jan and Mark,
remember?

IT WAS A HOLIDAY

It was a holiday, but we turned away from the holiday.
Books lay on the table, we didn't read them now.
In the distance was the great world, a world of love and betrayal,
unknown, unnamed, always, still completely new.
Those whom we'd known since childhood walked beside us
in silence, some vanished abruptly,
with a brief cry of fear—
like swallows, who are always frantic.
We were tired, but no one complained.
Nights were short, the dawns were transparent,
at evening orioles wept in the woods,
but we knew the streets and parks better.
We wandered slowly, looking carefully around us,
noting words in our memory—we thought:
we'll have to write them down later.
We held hands, wading through the sand
of abandoned suburbs. Heavy trains
passed before us in the distance,
the ocean roared, and darkness.

ALSO VITA CONTEMPLATIVA

IN THE TRAIN TO WARSAW

It can happen anywhere, sometimes in a train,
when I'm nowhere: suddenly the door
opens and forgotten figures enter,
my little nephew, who no longer is,
but approaches cheerful, laughing,
and a certain Chinese poet, who loved
the leaves of autumn trees and music,
theology students from Córdoba, still beardless,
emerge from nothingness and leap into view,
resuming their debate on God's attributes,
and splendid life surges like a waterfall in spring,
until at last a ringtone sounds, importunate,
then another, and a third, and all this great, strange world
contracts and vanishes, exactly like a field mouse,
who, sensing danger, draws adroitly into
its secret apartments.

IF I WERE TOMAŽ ŠALAMUN

If I were Tomaž Šalamun,
I'd always be happy, I think.
I'd dance on the Small Market Square until all hours
to a melody no one could place.
I'd play Mahler's Fifth gaily on the accordion.

What's the use, I'm an introvert,
who returns books late to the library
and sometimes envies life's heroes—
the bronzed lifeguards on August's beaches.
I could go on.

But one thing is certain: I'm not Tomaž Šalamun.
Tomaž came blessed with two imaginations,
Slovenian and Mexican, and he juggles them
with heart-stopping swiftness,

while I'm an eternal student of stenography,
struggling to understand how death enters the house
and how it leaves, and then returns,
and how it is defeated by a small freckled girl
reciting Dante from memory

—though I also seek the flame of rapture
pretty much everywhere, even in the budget theater,
the train, and almost every café
(but more unites than divides us).

If I were Tomaž Šalamun,
I'd ride wild on an invisible bicycle,
like a metaphor sprung from a poem's cage,
still not certain of its freedom,
but making do with movement, wind, and sun.

I LOOK AT A PHOTOGRAPH

I look at a photograph of the city where I was born,
at its lush gardens and winding streets, at the hills,
the Catholic roofs, the domes of Orthodox churches,
where on Sunday the basses sing so mightily
that neighboring trees sway as in a hurricane;
I gaze at the photograph, I can't tear my eyes away,
and suddenly I imagine that they're all still alive
as if nothing had happened, they still scurry to lectures,
wait for trains, take sky-blue trams,
check calendars with alarm, step on scales,
listen to Verdi's arias and their favorite operetta,
read newspapers that are still white,
live in haste, in fear, are always late,
are a bit immortal, but don't know it,
one's behind with the rent, another fears consumption,
a third can't finish his thesis on Kant,
doesn't understand what things are in themselves,
my grandmother still goes to Brzuchowice carrying
a cake on her outstretched arms and they don't droop,
in the pharmacy a shy boy requests a cure for shyness,
a girl examines her small breasts in a mirror,
my cousin goes to the park straight from his bath

and doesn't guess that soon he'll catch pneumonia,
enthusiasm erupts at times, in winter yellow lamps
create cozy circles, in July flies loudly celebrate
the summer's great light and hum twilit hymns,
pogroms occur, uprisings, deportations,
the cruel Wehrmacht in becoming uniforms,
the foul NKVD invades, red stars
promise friendship but signify betrayal,
but they don't see it, they almost don't see it,
they have so much to do, they need
to lay up coal for winter, find a good doctor,
the unanswered letters grow, the brown ink fades,
a radio plays in the room, their latest buy, but they're
still wearied by ordinary life and death,
they don't have time, they apologize,
they write long letters and laconic postcards,
they're always late, hopelessly late,
the same as us, exactly like us, like me.

WRITING POEMS

Writing poems is a duel
that no one wins—on one side
a shadow rises, massive as a mountain range
viewed by a butterfly, on the other,
only brief glimpses of brightness,
images and thoughts like a match flame
on the night when winter is born in pain.
It's trench warfare, a coded telegram,
long watching, patience,

a sinking ship that sends out signals
and stops sinking, a cry of triumph,
loyalty to the old, silent masters,
calm contemplation of a brutal world,
explosive joy, ecstatic, unsatisfied,
regret, everything passes, hope, nothing is lost,
a conversation without a final word,
a long break at school when the students
are gone, the defeat of one weakness

and the start of another, endless waiting
for the next poem, a prayer, mourning

for a mother, a momentary truce,
complaints and whispers in a charred confessional,
rebellion and magnanimous forgiveness,
squandering the whole estate, remorse, assent,
sprint and stroll, irony, cold gaze,
profession of faith, diction, haste,
the cry of a child who's lost his greatest treasures.

THE GREEN WINDBREAKER

When my father strolled through Paris,
often in the green windbreaker
that he had ordered tailor-made
(one of the few luxuries
in his rather modest life),
when he spent long hours in the Louvre,
studying the paintings of Corot and other lesser
masters from centuries past,
I didn't yet know, I couldn't know,
how much destruction lay hidden
in the years just then approaching,
as if that green windbreaker
brought him ill luck,
but now I begin to recognize,
to suspect that catastrophe
had been stitched into all his clothing,
regardless of color or shape,
and even the greatest master painters
could give him no assistance here.

WANDERING

We were vacationing with friends: a writer from the States,
whose poems measure justice, and an actor
from Warsaw, his face open to both good and evil guests;
it was in a sheer, deep valley of the young Rodan,
a sweltering late August day, one of those days
when autumn wakens from its catnap in the forest's depths.
We tried to find the spot we remembered
so clearly from the photo—the proud tower, secluded,
full of solitude, elegies, and sonnets, poetry's tower,

but new suburbs surrounded us,
white houses, and cars
as clean as a bureaucrat's conscience;
children walked their dogs,
dogs walked their adults,
in gardens roses awaited
the gardener's shears.

We were among friends, bees frantically
built frail walls for their winter homes,
on mild, musing hillsides wine was gathered

like a crimson mountain stream, embankments of wild dreams.
We made our pilgrimage to Rilke's tower,
which had become a strange cathedral,
and our journeying, seeking, wandering
seemed almost blissful, joyous uncertainty, bewilderment
revived us, was benign, even crucial,

and when at last, after a long while,
we found the tower
just as it had been in the photo,
uncertainty vanished,
and only stones remained,
wildflowers, friendship,
and the light ash of melancholy.

SILHOUETTES

MR. SOBERTIN, MR. ROMER—

THEY EXISTED, THEY LIVED

Suddenly memory's gate trembled and I saw a cart,
rural ash trees: I caught the sweet scent of horse droppings.
It was summer, stubble fields, a mountain stream, an osier
    above it.
A kingfisher made its entrance like a Hollywood star.
Mama in a light-blue dress, probably from before the war.
I saw Mr. Sobertin picking flowers on the meadow
(Mr. Sobertin was the platonic idea of an old bachelor).
I saw refugees. I knew outcasts, widowers.
I tended to dismiss fortune's favorites.
When it comes to victims, each is different
(defeat is an individual substance).

R thinks I was born too late. "Nothing was left."
I remember Edmund Romer well, a cartographer's son;
he made friends with my parents, I liked him.
The past trailed after him, Lvov, ghosts,
and maps, dotted with white stains and a little blood
(black and rusty blotches, long since dry).

Nothing was left—you can't say that!

The door of memory and expectation opens.

Fishing ponds open at dusk.

The hazy silhouettes of exiles drift on the bank,

and swallows, crying loudly, cut the last connections' threads.

GALCZYNSKI, OF COURSE

I listen to Saint-Saëns's Requiem and think about poetry.
It's August, the wind wrestles the trees
and yellow bindweed blossoms in suburban hedges.

You were my parents' favorite poet,
they didn't read much poetry otherwise.
What drew them to your books?

They must have liked the humor, the risky
jokes of a cautious artist:
"too much wind for my wool,"

and the funny name of your company, "Terror
& Tummy," a firm that thrived
even in times of the greatest terror.

A light touch and brashness, and disarming charm,
right? My parents were completely different,
they lacked the talents you possessed

in such abundance—but I think
they wanted to rescue what they'd been—I don't know
what to call it, that unseen something

that runs through your poems too,
but well concealed, deeply hidden
like the gold coin under a miser's mattress,

the stubborn, ardent striving that is
the whisper of great poetry and may become
the quiet, patient hymn of life.

THE RHÔNE VALLEY

High walls, sheer and powerful.
All New York could fit here,
along with its airports
and its city of underground hallways.
But the Rhône doesn't wait for comparisons,
it flows swiftly, drunk on its own youth.
The vineyards are more cautious—they never rush,
they lie on hillsides, placid as the Swiss.
While the clouds travel on to Italy, to Bergamo,
to Padua and Ravenna—crossing borders.
The valley contains memory,
gray as stones, as granite.
The young Rhône rushes to the sea
but thoughts move in the opposite direction.
Streams fall endlessly
in white robes of mist
as imagination, like a solitary climber,
battles daily with the force of gravity.
The old masters still live here,
unrecognizable, under assumed names,
in modest houses, little gardens;
you may catch sight of them in summer evenings,

when lazy bonfires blaze
—they tend bees and hollyhocks,
naive like Le Douanier Rousseau.
You and I are silent, attending the night.
It takes us even higher than the Alps.

PAINTINGS

FOR ZBYLUT GRZYWACZ

Countless paintings hung on the walls
of the apartment on Krakow Street. (Why
Krakow Street in Krakow? The city
didn't know how to get home?)

None of it matters now—
the names of streets, your patriotic passion
for Kazimierz, your loyal photos
of old houses, dilapidated gates.

Even that apartment is gone now.
On canvases: human faces, women's bodies,
gray and pink, the world's yellow stains.
Drawings and sketches of acts, studies of aging,

natures mortes, some dust-covered
and doubly dead, others fresh
as fruit at market stands, gleaming
in June's remembered light.

In summer light strikes objects
directly, while in winter it hides
lazily in wardrobes, sleeps on the stove,
like minerals on museum shelves.

A champion talker, a fan of Caravaggio,
you vanished after a few months of illness,
of suffering and strength in dying.
Paintings and friendship remain,

canvases, which don't understand
their loneliness, their dusk,
and friendship, which of course
lives on—but as a widow now.

MY FATHER NO LONGER KNOWS ME

My father no longer knows me. Not even
those sparks of consciousness
that cheered us not so long ago.
He lies submerged in darkness, sleeps, dozes,
as if he'd already taken leave.
There are still the brief moments, though,
when his real face is revealed.

CLOUD

Poets build a home for us—but they themselves
can't dwell in it
(Norwid in the poorhouse, Hölderlin in a tower).

At dawn mist above the forest,
a journey, the rooster's husky call,
the hospitals are shut, uncertain signals.

At noon we sit in a café on the square,
we observe the azure sky
and a laptop's azure screen;

a plane writes out the pilot's manifesto
in clear, white script,
perfectly legible to the farsighted.

Azure is a color that happily
promises great events,
and then sits back and waits.

A leaden cloud draws close,
terrified pigeons rise
gracelessly into the air.

Storms and hailstones gather
in dark streets and squares,
and yet the light doesn't die.

Poets, invisible like miners,
hidden in the shafts,
build a home for us:

lofty rooms rise
with Venetian windows,
splendid palaces,

but they themselves
can't dwell in it:

Norwid in the poorhouse, Hölderlin in a tower;
the jet's lonely pilot
hums a lullaby; awaken, Earth.

IN VALLEYS

And the lovely Garonne, which passes
through drowsy villages each night
like a priest with the last sacrament.
Dark clouds grow in the sky.
The Visigoths live on, in certain faces.
In summer the empire of insects spreads.
You consider how not to be yourself:
is it only on journeys, in valleys,
which open others' wounds?
In a bookshop the sales clerk calls
the author of *To the Lighthouse*
Virginia. As if she might
turn up at any minute, on a bicycle,
with her long, sad face.
But Paul Valéry (of the Academy) thought
history didn't exist. Perhaps he was right.
Perhaps we've been taken in. When he was dying,
General de Gaulle tried to find him
penicillin. Too late.

KINGS

I'M A STUDENT

Those were days when I walked around a little hungry,
a little dazed, and desire spoke to me
violently. A little lonely,
slightly happy, a bit the actor of myself,
I listened to music, the music was wild,
I admired the Renaissance palaces,
I visited our poor kings
at Wawel Castle and tried to comfort them
and stretched the truth; for all that, though, they
put fingers to their pale lips
and counseled silence. It was winter,
snow smothered the flowers, and the voice
of destiny could not speak soon.
So it was. Woolen gloves. Amen.

SELF-PORTRAIT

MAY 2008, AFTER SEEING

ERIC FISCHL'S SELF–PORTRAIT

Keeps growing older. Frayed costumes. Reads a lot,
    sometimes vanishes
in books like Indians in trackless jungles. Repeats himself,
everything repeats, yellow notebook in his pocket, music's
    great summons.
Evenings he moves to the window in a rumpled shirt and
    yawns.
Looks a little different in each picture—his father's face
invades his own, slightly melancholy face; the short white
    beard,
his enemies insist, must signify capitulation.
The eyes gaze at the lens with hope. Growing older.

Likes water, flat sleepy rivers, and the green ocean:
swimming, his body disappears in the dark currents
as if temporarily testing another mode of being.
The wind takes his breath, night bestows absolute peace
(the only absolute we've got, a friend scoffs,

they've been arguing for a decade).
A citizen, he thinks of his injured country,
the garden of a childhood that never was.

Takes many trips—April in Belgrade, the pockmarks of a
    recent war,
the swollen Danube recalls its carefree early years in Germany;
Jerusalem in May, more scars of war, but holiness
drifts above the mythic city like the scent of magnolias.
A journalist's questions seem oddly familiar.
Strangeness grows. Always the same: early breakfast, after
    lunch
a long stroll. Slowly becoming a fixed object.
Dreams drag him underground, dawn deftly rescues him.

But it is I, still I, ever searching
and shapeless, always I, every morning opens
a shining new chapter and can't finish it, it is I,
on the street, at the station, I hearing a child's cry, students
    laughing,
a starling's shriek, the I of ignorance, uncertainty, desire,
expectation, and wild joy, the I who understands nothing,
answers insults, hesitates, starts afresh,
guards himself in conversations, in despair, in learned debates,

in a winter day's quiet, it is I, bored, resigned,
unhappy, haughty, it is I, daydreaming
like a teenager, dead tired like the aged,
I in the museum, at the seashore, on Krakow's main square,
yearning for a moment that won't show, that hides
like mountain peaks on cloudy afternoons, brightness
finally arrives, and I suddenly know all, know it is not I.

MAY, THE BOTANIC GARDEN

REMEMBERING PROFESSOR

ANDRZEJ JANKUN

In May at the Botanic Garden
day and night
the frenzied work never relents—
all the plants, vast
trees and tiny ferns
rush to put on
their finest outfits
as if heading out to take
graduation exams.

CARTS

Carts full of hay
abandoned the town
in greatest quiet.

Cautious glances from the curtains.

A morning empty as a waiting room.

The rustling of papers in the archives;
men calculate the losses.

But that world.
Suitcases packed.
Sing for it, oriole,
dance for it, little fox,
catch it.

ACKNOWLEDGMENTS

Grateful acknowledgment is made to the following publications, in which these poems originally appeared:

The Atlantic: "The Last Stop"

The Believer: "Kings"

Granta: "New Hotel"

Harper's Magazine: "If I Were Tomaž Šalamun"

Harvard Review: "Improvisation," "Luxembourg Gardens"

The Hedgehog Review: "Also *Vita contemplativa*," "Impossible," "Metaphor," "Not Thinking About Aesthetics"

The Kenyon Review: "Café," "Self-Portrait," "*Vita contemplativa*," "Wandering"

Little Star: "And the Lovely Garonne," "Falling Asleep over a Volume of Cavafy," "It Was a Holiday," "Leonardo," "Like the King of Asini," "Music of the Lower Spheres," "Mute City," "Silhouettes"

The New Republic: "Carts," "Family Home," "Unwritten Elegy for Krakow's Jews"

The New York Review of Books: "Now That You've Lost Your Memory," "Self-Portrait in a Little Museum"

The New Yorker: "In Valleys"

Orion: "Swifts Storming St. Catherine's Church"

A Public Space: "Lost"

Slate: "About My Mother," "3 Arkonska Street"

The Threepenny Review: "Defenseless," "Out Walking with My Father"

Tin House: "Cloud," "I Look at a Photograph," "Joseph Street"

.